THE COUPLE WHO FELL TO EARTH

MICHELLE BITTING

POEMS

For Elijah and Vera Rose

…and at the midnight hour
to talk with the clock by tapping a wall
in the solitary confinement of the universe.

—VERA PAVLOVA

hic Rhodus, hic salta

—AESOP

THE COUPLE WHO FELL

TO EARTH

EARTH

Because I'd forgotten
I'd shoved that wrinkled bulb
into a slit of dubious soil last winter,
just as I'd lost sight of it
buried under a decade of rust and oil
in the garage we haven't cleaned
since the summer our daughter
was born. Some seasons prove
more hazardous than others
and one wind-thrashed night,
I groped for a stray cigarette
from the grime atop
the busted refrigerator we use to store
light bulbs and toilet paper,
slipped my fingers into a filthy halo
of booster seats
and nursing pillows,
formula bottles and plastic bathing tub
and pulled out a crumpled baggie
of bulbs. Now the garden gnome
winks through a lattice cross
of immaculate light,
so smug in his weird cone hat
and Santa coat, his bed
of broad conceptions: stigma and stamen,
the once frozen loam
having cracked like an egg,
the stone exterior unrolled,
the barracks collapsed
and out slithered this serpent

of a single red bloom
like a prisoner climbing the roof
of the impossible panopticon
and lighting a match to herself,
becomes a flag of fire
in the moon's glowing lake. Goodnight!
Death had not dominion, after all. If Christ rose
no one really knows
how he managed to wade through
all that festering, flying from tomb
to feathered clouds, do they?
Beauty needs no apology.
We could never explain
the crumbling citadel transformed
to Easter morning goody
basket—blue lace and tangerine
jelly beans, nor the scary bunny
heads my husband and I sometimes wore,
spitting bitter carrots
into the whites of each other's eyes.
The garden is a Chagall
guarded by worms
in the vaults of subterranean ruins. The horses,
delirious from so long
in the desert of no water,
their mouths turn to mines
of glittering salt and make pictures.
A woman wakes and sees
a girl wandering the yard,
remembers hiding treasure once
and pretending to find it

as if for the first time, as if
pulling a bouquet from
the barrel of a hat, from slugs
and dirt, the miserable bottom:
your darkest places imaginable.

THE COUPLE WHO FELL TO EARTH

We went flying without a map
as naked astronauts often do.
The borders of our bodies
blended into one, an erosion
of planets and vaporized stars,
we hurtled through space
and burned up entering.
Please forgive this clumsy beauty,
no more than grains of dust,
moon debris, a streak of light.
We land and make a circle,
a cornucopia in the crop
and the heat of our hips
bores down, carving a cradle,
the perilous pit,
the stone fruit heart
of human fire. The body
loves what it loves
and we can't stop it;
we become an O around,
we become the snake itself,
the rosetta coil, the upper room.
We are flag and stigmata,
the ship set sail, the smoking
orifice, the holy divot
and buried cup. Lips
to each other's eyes,
we will seal our demons in,
the flowering trees
and muddy gardens

of our Eden-scorched mouths. Crowns
tossed to the breeze,
the honeycomb bleeding gold
and queen's poison darts.
We have watched
the fountain grass,
felt their glowing spines
shoot through us,
the mournful wheat heads
made of glass
trace a cross
on the cistern tomb.
And to think we slept
through it all, though
the dream kept smacking us
with every surge
of the sea's cold blade.
We are the lion
and the lamb, the tooth
in the flesh, flaming halo
and silken curl,
the wounded bird
and coming ecstasy,
this kingdom we've built
till death do us part.

THE GOODS

It's the corporeal feelings
I crave the most: aridity, lust,
their aches' redaction, love-weariness,
kiss-quest, falling in bed again
when loneliness breaks a sweat
and we mount a horse
called faith borne
on this wheel of March,
charge and stamping
heat of the noble
night that will carry us,
tongue and thigh
entwined and shuddering
against our own coming history.

RECYCLED COLISEUM

That gray lump of clay skulked
in a wicker corner of the kitchen
more than a week before my hands
would have at it. So much
to take down first—decaying arches,
old roles long played
in the family crypt. In between, there were soups
to brew for aging parents,
the dreadful meats they'd trained
me to hunt. So much to clean,
toxic-free. Who will explain this?
I'm no sculptor, void of required skills,
more a wrangler of raw softness, devastated waste.
When the moment to make came,
I had faith the gnashing exotics
would outsmart their chains,
toss off rusted links and cuffs.
Just a matter of when.
I kept going as they rose up,
bared tusks and claws,
a sea of furrowed manes and exoskeletons
under wobbly arenas. Not knowing
which would prove more crucial—time
or materials—I threw myself to the kitchen
floor and forced gaunt palms
to gray flame, earthly oblivion,
taking as cue to begin
when the radio clicked on, streaming
tales of The Fifty Years War. Everything's
a sign or corrosive, even the sun

will turn book covers white as senators' robes
whispering down damp arcades. Now the gladiator
takes to the stage. Five pale fingers curled
together into a fist as the crowd
roars on. To thrust and then unfurl,
merciful as flowers, flying. Strands of silt
I tear to make something bare, entirely new. Lit up
in the end, you'll see one shape: a home,
minus the killing but made from the dead.

NEMESIS NECKLACE

Sometimes you have to wear one,
wrap the strands of glowing
green around yourself, air

the grave beads loudly
about shoulder and neck. The self's
shady Daguerreotype

coming to surface
through exposure to light. Bitumen
and lavender oil, apertures

for beating moth wings
so truth may be made
visible after dwelling

in dim-lit spaces. The way
Aunt Mary's sweaters smelled
of death and peppermint,

White Shoulders perfume bottle
with damsel cameo etching
I'd chat up in the bathroom

before returning to what geriatric fuzz
we'd fallen into. From all doldrums
of hell are heroes borne. Even

the terrorist's shoes fit feet
just like your own. Bones shaped
like Superman's cape. Friends and foes,

how often did Nietzsche imagine himself
wearing Wagner's robes,
the better to glimpse his beloved Cosima

stepping naked from her bath,
sobbing for what he coveted
down the path of insanity? Like

those suitors were to Odysseus,
slashed battalions
of so much chimera, mirrors

held up to reflect fields of cruel flowers
felled under a red sun
so Penelope could rise to the throne

of his one-eyed monster?
Oh sea...
let me wrap my darkest me

in your drape of flame and sapphire,
my arms raised to night:
whatever it takes

to conduct this flight, the moon's music
tearing the silence
where I inevitably fall

and never mind the drowning.
Where my pendant heart gleams
beneath grassy cliffs

and opaque plummet,
the drowsy waves that beckon
as the lighthouse sways

between the buttons,
beaming its code
from a conflicted core

that warns: it's not
always becoming
to follow yourself home.

GOLD SILK SPIDERS

From Madagascar, so fond of spinning, humidity, heat. What's inside is
what's coveted: coiled treasure, a noble interior. Sometimes the female
bodies—silver carapaces—millions of them, fastened in place with
intricate machinery, cough up strands of silk for weaving into cloth and
the prices won on fashion blocks for sticky web-woven robes. I saw a
program about it, watched a model draped in folds of the spider-finery
float down a runway like a human sun, her arms outstretched, Christ-like.
As kids we were grilled on Sunday nights, the family table an interrogation
meant to draw out moneyed answers and better manners. *Whose face is on
the hundred-dollar bill?* he'd ask, clamping teeth to fork, his fist set firmly
down while beneath my pink napkin something tensed to spring: *Ben
Franklin!* from the glowing lap of myself—I Heimliched that shit right
up, my jellied innards trembling like a new, wet colt and imagine father's
shock handing over the green. Imagine the skills required. Imagine
skeins of spooled history spilling, arachnid shells crumbled across fine,
metallic tables. In Marin, California, women kill themselves having run
out of what keeps bodies humming before husbands throw them over
for younger clones. More than a few melancholy moms hunkered above
porcelain, uncoiling their insides to better fit a daughter's designer jeans.
I open my mouth and yellow songs fall out. Calls of salvation, emaciated
praise. The skills required to pull it from yourself, chameleons crawling,
bug-eyed, in the grass beside. And that banana-hued beauty, Nephila
Clavipes, on her eight evil legs, the Midas center streaming, screaming to
be touched: holy, golden, killer strong. Surpassing even Kelvin—material
used in the making of bullet-proof vests.

BEGINNINGS

When Job stands up to God
the poems tumble out.
Like the sun sees itself
wrenched from the horizon,

I know the best time to make
remains this fragile ledge
between dark and day.
I wake up early

and tread a thin precipice:
crank of stove's green knob,
the click, click, click
of a half-turn to the left

and the pilot lets
blue flames roar.
               Auroras
in the domestic universe, iron flecks

falling into the gurgle
coalesce in a hot void, an unseen
industry of color,
the teakettle womb. This is the moment

I know myself best,
the rest still hard at dreaming
in rooms light years away.
An empty kitchen

where I've come to slap
my handprints on the walls:
paper, scissors, rock,
a child's game of concealment

and revelation
like in the caves of Chauvet Pont-d'Arc,
where you have to not mind
breathing trails

of poison gas
exhaled from weeping roots:
trees in the limestone veil.
Where you have to walk

a cool humidity and silence
like a creature being stalked,
animals uncaged
in the auteur's cradle

scraping charcoal over stone.
                    Where
you have to stand at a distance
but close enough to be overwhelmed by

the prehistoric shape
of lions fighting in the sky.

DRESSED UP LIKE HOLMES FALLING
INTO A GLASS DARKLY

What was I looking for
all those Februarys ago,
lost in the cave of my parents' garage, peering down
the lens of a mail-order microscope,
sex of blue milk
and simmered grasses, a blobby iridescence
smeared on five & dime slides. While
rafters swelled with foul-smelling vapors,
winter flexed its god-big muscles,
gray beams of fractured light
demolishing the clouds' easy geometry,
cotton babes unswaddled by tempests,
their eyes poked through
into stunned recognition—windows
to star soot beyond. Watson, let's not pretend
we aren't chained to the past. The smartest sleuths in town
know it's a spiral, not a circle
unlocking the skeleton path, the caverns
of looms—nymphs and burning honey
stitched in tempered gold—a hive
of purple bees. And I swear,
I swear in the future
I won't mention that man in the corner,
his relentless ablutions
and fonts of whiskey, weary pieta
of a dead son draped
forever across his lap. How the scene begets
a thirsty daughter, this moony detective
with the jaws of a man

and a monocle raised to music
swelling in the fog. I've got my deerstalker cap,
my lily gloves, my brain wrapped tight
in a houndstooth coat, daggers
and revolvers tucked inside the membrane
folds, high—octane solutions
cradling my veins. And you,
trusty consort, right there reading the signs,
the cryptic case on cue—face of a clock,
strung from the Mother hip,
the heart that spins inside—all the beautiful murders
and numbered hands you point to,
saying, *See here, Holmes,*
we've all the time in the world.

And I pull myself out
by the ears of a dangling rabbit,
my many-colored silks,
spiral bleed of roses
tossed at the feet
of the sweating matador, dusty
in his coat. Where
the sun beats down,
the crowd cheers
and a thin white handkerchief
flutters in the stands,
making a little breeze
for the child who watches the ring
from the shade of her mother's side,
bewitched by the muscular dance,
these near-death misses,
red cape swirl
lifting and falling
in the heat of Las Ventas, Madrid.

RESENTMENT IS A HARD HABIT TO BREAK

To cast off, finally, all that anguish about the father, corners of the mouth
slunk down, the mind turned seaward, nowhere but south. To beg pardon,
break the scathing, critical seals. What is freedom? A forehead caressed,
fingers oiled, touched to clove, lavender, ash, the self marked one's own
forever. Remember that kindergarten class where you subbed and a girl
with gold curls and maniac's laugh pressed her drawing to your face —
some weird lopsided caftan scribbled in green: *It's so evil you can't even
get into it!* She cackled and tore off. The door to this church is heavy
and hard to enter. The arms of certain loved ones, hard to enter. What
happened in paradise when the father refused you now commands a
common misery. Christmas mornings moping under tinsel, unhappy
manic on his sofa as you rent red ribbons off Bullocks-Wilshire boxes, the
havoc of never enough. When font water burns, nails and wood will sing
relief. Everything turned on its head, feet crested, un-rooted, up. Best to
reckon how a house divided against itself and falling unfolds a warped
radiance, wings of a shiny beast stomping off, circled in smoke. Time to
sweep the burnt parts and head home, make some twirling mobile of it.
The lark, her numbers drilled down, still terribly bright — gorgeous stories
wrested from wreaked disaster. Like dazzling Aphrodite divined spells
to turn a lover's hair to snakes, or a daughter into a harlot hell bent on
sleeping with the man who most resembles her father.

THE MOMENT OF POSSIBLE FUTURES

If we swim back to the place
where the road fanned out, fork ourselves
and make five prongs: Mom, Dad, Me,
The Painter and Baby Bro
parting ways at the crossroads, pretend
I set them on their bikes, their
skateboards, high heels and work boots,
each with a hobo sack of snacks
for the journey: tuna, Jack Daniels, pot brownies, and Ritz,
where would we ride to?
You can stare through the glass
of the aquarium tank
where clown-colored fish jockey for position,
note imperial feeders and bottom sloths — one
resembling the bloated soul
someone posted last week when I said
He looks like a horse and that must be why he's sad.
Fitting in doesn't suit me
but I've learned to exist
on ambrosia made of stories,
the swirling banister of clouds that make
the sky a staircase to *there*. Sky that says: *Enter me,*
sustenance of steps
shaped from vapor and light.
I spin myself and my family cell with it,
separate yet one
in a flesh no longer monstrous,
the menagerie where, finally, no keeper
lords over the kingdom of time.

GOLD RING

The one with big and small diamonds
        on my left ring finger
                belonged to Grandma
        everybody comments on it
quite stunning
        and kind of ugly, too
                the way a grandma ring can be
        a bit clunky and overwrought
the gems have a story
        the grubby tiny ones
                from their original engagement
        on the California coast
north of Malibu
        that place where two giant rocks
                come to a head
        and the surf tumbles around
the gods inside
        at war with each other
                he said, *I love you, Doll*
        he said that
and how could she not answer?
        all they had
                this thing they were making up
        other stones came
from a wedding band
        one for each anniversary
                (their 25th, their 50th)
        the large "bling" jewels
you could say
        and all of it

34

deconstructed, reconstructed
like marriage goes
bound up
in one crazy sculpture
when she died
he gave it to me
we stood in the blue bedroom
where she took the last terrible gasps
sailed off
on a sea of silent dreams
he opened the drawer and said
Seventy five years, seventy-five years
I don't know what I'll do
without her
and pressed the ring
into my palm
all that preciousness
my grandpa never talked much
until she got sick
and then I visited regularly
though she hardly knew me anymore
he was glad for the company
and the words tumbled out
now I come all the time
we sit in his backyard
talking about birds
about his roses
he tends with such care
and the bright red feeder
swinging over our heads

glitters in the sun
its perfect geometry
sugar and water mixed
for the hummingbirds
the moment they sip
so sweet they can't resist
coming back for more

HEART

WITH TAKE ANOTHER LITTLE PIECE OF MY HEART NOW, BABY BLARING ON THE CAR RADIO

And the dashboard flashing its round yellow light
two miles outside town,
I can see my tires need air
                                        but which one?

Sometimes the heart has too much air

or not enough. So I stop,
squeeze the pump,
wrestle the gust
and gasp. What if more
                                sucks out?

What if reckless backfires? What if
this is Lorca's highway...

to take the wrong turn

and that coyote crying in the hills
plans to make me a midnight meal?

There's never fair warning
just this steady state
                                of famished

and time, our preferred prey,
darting under rough brush.

The thickest parts.

My heart
a flashlight. My heart
a scythe
a switchblade,
slashing my own tires,

                    to see what happens,

to hear bones
grinding over
stripped down struts,
brash disaster. I could watch these wheels
                                burn around

for a hundred years
                        gliding over
                            the perilous edge,

over and over, my love roams
an abandoned road
        and I wave back

                        bloody pages,
that alarm clock
coyote, one step behind,
sniffing
        red entrails

my dirty feet drag

        stamped in perfect heart-shaped prints.

IN THE MINING SHAFT

The ladder down is rickety
and swoons, each rung a bent bow
under heel. The air thickens;
its black dream seethes. Mansion
of many dooms, chained doors
quicken, rupture breath
as the lamp-heart flickers, a yellow bird
swaying in sync. I don't know
what I'm looking for, only know
it is more precious
than coal or gold. Some days
I think I won't clock out,
won't heed the weakening canaries,
resurrect or compose myself
in that cold, dim light. I'm lost
if I am anything. Deaf
to whistles, the land-lark cry, click
of my empty lunch pail,
its skull licked clean.

Because I can no longer see without them,
I keep my spectacles close to my heart.

Magnified, the heart sees everything
along with the blind. To lose my glasses

means it all goes blurry, my breath knocked out
and then the door jimmies open. Eternity will be

claimed by a burning cup, fresh from the embers
and grasped without touching. Eye candy,

the tangible and spectered, occupying 99%.
Spirit oil slathered from one frayed corner

to the Other. Take this as a starting point:
Allah, Yahweh, God...and scroll down, graphite

and trees we circle on our knees, throats
exposed as baby chicks. A cool arrangement,

an acrylic consensus, hung in the Louvre
where we huddle, moshing it out. Silver

and gold, silver and gold. Lawyers, guns
and dildos: bring it. True believers

hide in attics, stretching fresh canvas,
praying for endless arias to sing back

big bank oblivion. No need to seek binoculars
or the Mona Lisa's grin. History's bullet-proof

agenda has already been written
across my mind's fugitive page.

THOUGHTS JOTTED IN A VICODIN HAZE ON A LINE BY WENDELL BERRY

—When despair for the world grows in me…

When despair for the world grows in me

there's a pill in my dresser

wrapped in layers of Chinese silk

I down

with a swig of pink lemonade.

On an empty stomach

it's pure:

LUCY IN THE SKY WITH DIAMONDS

though sometimes bent over the toilet

I think

maybe it's time for a new obsession?

So cruise to the café

and presto…

It's you!

scouting table space

with your writer's blur and hunch

bedraggled by deadlines…

but fine, you say
showing me your hand, the eczema
not so bad now, see?
with the aid of a new-age healer
not exactly believed in
you being from Brooklyn
and therefore conflicted
by which I mean
it troubles me
to see you suffer (cracked skin, powdery flaky nail irritation with fissures
mangling the elegant natural anatomy)

and yet

it provides such an excellent excuse

to touch your hand…

Is a brief examination in order?

                    (this doctor's always in)

well   enough   now

        with your affliction

let's talk about

    addiction

              the ululating tick

     of my mind's swaddled clock

           my pillow tongue

sawed

     your jagged radiance   today

and the peace of wild things

     restored

         pharmaceutically
come here

            I want to touch it

I'm a star-congested stream, love-struck jamboree

your hand   a spangled oar

rowing me along

the fringe

of dangerous water…

IN THE BEGINNING, SOMEWHAT ELEVATED

It's 7 AM, my eyes
have opened and you

are everywhere. I'm
a gnarl, a knot,

an orb: heavy metal
pin-balling down

a road paved in gold.

Accept me. I love the dawn.
The sun is a sea

I throw myself into,
iced radiance

panicking my breath
clean out. Herodotus said

he knew the sick
by their dreams

until reason came
to poison the heart,

the surgeon's scalpel
finally unearthing

its bloody whereabouts.

Not me.
I've been sleeping in a forest

ever since you came around.
I wander an irrational

matrix, golem
brothers singing out,

mistaking trunks
for snug caskets.

I thread the interior
and the whole green toy

lights up, a mechanical quilt
that tilts

as I finger
its bark facade.

Some see the morning as a curse,
the first shards of light,

a dropped spoon
down the gullet

of a drain.

But I see the body
rising from satin amnesia

becoming a fist, a fish
that swims

through darkness
swallowing stars.

THEN I LET YOU GO

With my wood and silver crosses
swinging from the rearview
with my lavender crystals
smoking in emerald crucibles
my heart, a paper scroll
a burning bird
a cindered testament
curling to ash
a form of nowhere
You see
I've rallied my armies
and still the red ants stream
forests drained
all manner of means
I change tacks
cross hellish waters
sometimes for centuries
and sailing back
recall dry land
a darkened theater
sitting next to you once
There were children
in rows around us
my elbow at rest
close to touching yours—how
can I keep this to myself?
Light from a screen
the cartoon characters
riot's delirium
studding my attention

hairs on my arm
ants in my hips
picking up your honeyed scent
making an unseen exodus
I think it was Madagascar
and all my slave girls
woke at once
up from their pillowed lofts
their pagan eyes
and hot palms
wiping the froth
bare toes shimmied
close to an edge
I could just make out
my deck sinking
as I counted down
to jump ship. Oh
say the word
and I'll swim home
walk this blue-quilted sea
I'm sewn into
me and the strange ones
our patchwork language
love spelled out
in buried channels
sunken stories
broken stones
too Greek
too wild for me
to ever know how to name

IMMANENT

IMMANENT, PURGATORIO
(WITH DANTE ALIGHIERI)

The sea takes our sorrows
and turns them back to joy
as the archer fingers her quiver,

making the mind move in reverse, her ploy:
grasp the burning arrow of unbelief;
aim for the whites of the future's story.

So that we might absolve our grief.
So that we might discern
the second beauty we have kept concealed,

the world being a jagged heaven my soles learn
to tread more tenderly. My head of red clouds
and wounded distortions: bells and satanic flutes heard

at hyper-pitch by the flea-bitten crowd.
These that, weeping, sent me to your side,
so you understand nothing where everything is allowed.

I broke the rules of myself open to find
experience lost to a religion that kept
me sweating under its shadowy rank and file.

Scars in cursive etched on my skull's swept
frontispiece dissolve when love bathes
every follicle in its hot oil treatment.

To know me is to salve me. Save
discretion for last. *Let pleasure be your guide.*
Your laughter and the lathe

of the moment shearing, light
that hides no evil as it grinds me round
to the bedrock of authenticity. Why

stumble a cobbled path, why bleed forgiveness down?
I set flame to my feet long ago
on route to a holy garden, compostable hours,

meaning a life fully played, fully flown. I throw
my body back and with mind unlatched remember
a brother and the tree he climbed, strung with avocados.

It wasn't yearning for pocked fruit per
se, only addiction to forks and his fall,
One was made with gold, the other silver:

the start of a long descent, drawn
by a twig that pierced the corner of his mouth
as he tumbled through sky, leaf and branch top, the drop

of blood that multiplied on concrete until I lost count.
Take care to wash away these wounds...
I would but I'm falling further, then being now.

He was painting the path crimson and swooned.
We shuffled him back towards home,
amazed by his bricoleur, his already groomed

talent for transforming pain to art, honed
in early childhood hours. *Unveil*
your lips, drive the devil from your bones.

I follow him down the spiraling tail,
I steer him towards his bitter end:
the frozen chains, the burning rail.

Here's the theater we sneak into again.
Ann Margaret's diamond-drunk and furred,
rolling on the floor. Beans spill from blue light. Can

you hear me? Can you see me peeling splendor,
the purged fruit, our long war dropped for metamorphosis?
I beat three times upon my breast asking her

to open out of mercy: Michelle. Your suicide sits
in heaven now, there was nothing more to be done.
Disease, a prickly past, yet, who can resist

ranting, the walking dead reanimated, one
foot weeping, the other lacing its rational boot?
I have cried and cursed you, run

my hands up the scaled tree, brute
in its quest to birth and strangle beauty,
a major and minor tune

mirrored in one twisting.
Listen. The moon's chariot glitters on the shore
past the place where my powers cannot see.

A mother masked darkly points her sickle towards
Elysium nonetheless, a skyline direction. Fooled,
we learn to know the limits of our gods, fickle stewards

in skill to raise us: guilty and good, honeyed, cruel:
a chaos of bees toiling the willful hive, meaning
only self-reflexivity will fuel

this plot towards its forested resolution. Sing
songs to the dead, place jewels of remorse
in the crown of revolution. Wings

grow from us, Brother, as we lead the horse
to its tired field and part ways. What hurt,
what iron rings manacled me, perforce,

to that infernal state, now converts
to cloud-fine matter, halo-akin,
dust-thin and glowing like the wreaths of Saturn.

Father, you see how it is:
grace no longer absent. You are
a shade passing along a singed horizon,

the porphyry blade of your mother
tongue turned to nuts and bolts
drives my myth-making machinery: art

and intellect through which, most
humbly, I've brought us to our knees.
In effigy: bodies circling the terrace boast

lantern-like flight. Ghosts float, the seas
bless them as they flicker and fold
seeds of flowers into the moon's lucent breast. Please

tell the ones who asked the angels who told
me to retire my bent towards calamity's green:
From this time on, love governs my soul.

The rest is mystery and history re-seen.

BODY

And a rush of halogen feathers flies out
from the moon's busted pillow,
I stand at the edge, Mother
and the pasture glowing
between us, stubbled crater
stabbed with bells
and icy nettles, once again,
begins to melt. A flock
of seagulls firing up
the red horizon
makes our horse much more distinct,
stomping around her bold
perimeter, dark as desire. She lifts
a single ankle
so I won't recognize the danger,
her language tucked
like diamond rooks
in the shadow of each hoof. She's come
a long way to find me,
the night's glass staircase
ground down
with rhythmic tramping,
quarry of stars
she's jacked over, rocks glittered,
the lunatic truth
and clashing call
of all those clapping, insomniac girls
you fought
and girls you taught
to make the message clear:
Every poem's a love poem
no matter how weary the world.

ELEGY FOR A BODY

There was a time I'd spend an afternoon
digging the bitter green sliver from a fair garlic thumb,
seed mountains of weepy Heirlooms, thread hunks
of yellow dough through a roller's metal teeth,
the long Rapunzel locks strung from one end
of our tiny kitchen to the other, then snipped off quick
into boiling fumes. Meanwhile, my baby suckled,
siphoning fuel, sheen of buttered stars poking through
my shirt's thin firmament; child I'd soon nurse to bed
only to get up three times in the night
and knowing that, I still had the juice to be cheerful,
to lift high the steaming nest of noodles,
to center that tangled gold on my husband's everyday plate
and everything about the moment slow motion focus
on his face: grateful; love rising through the numbness,
melting the day's cold. He'd look up at me, at his food
and lean closer into that delicious heat,
his mouth a flower flamed open by the sun.

A GENTLE REMINDER

When the electricity between us crimped
becoming a tender fist
of crossed wires, a wise man said
Keep pouring the milk
and we did. With ghosts in tow:
father in his lumberjack boots
and Swiss Army Knife
pressed to psychic circuitry,
what layers remained were shaved
to core and copper filament. Bone
threads run through clavicle
animating my neck
involuntarily. You in red clown nose
and polka dot tie.
What we do to survive,
masks of mermaid colors
to ward off ancestral gloom. Traveling,
we found sand from the Caribbean
matched synagogue floors
enticing children to the basement
where they once prayed, staying
silent. In the sun above surface
every crack reveals its true nature.
Pretend to love
whatever prophet you're told,
avoid the Auto Da Fe
at all costs. The future brings
a babe in basket
navigating strange mires.
Lovers hide their light

underground, singing
the passion
of *Bare ruined choirs.*

MORNING AT THE CAFÉ VIDA

And it begins to rain
lightly on the plein air seating

so that agile busboys
hustle wet tables

under dry awnings, surfaces specked
with tiny drops like shattered salt

on marble tops, ground fine. I like
a lot of flavor on my food,

especially Fleur de Sel
from the Guerande region

of France, but not when we fight
this way on Valentine's Day,

words like Fleurs Du Mal
flung from nowhere

like the bad news recently
that out of twenty-two students

from my fifth grade class,
three have committed suicide.

See, life gets stuck,
trapped granules sour

between cheek and gums,
searing a tender, unseen wound,

a sudden swelling
of nerves and throat — pain

and teeth overrun with damp,
the ship and chandeliers going under.

One minute we're waltzing,
veils of love unlaced

so delicately, the ballroom
of another day picking up

kids and phone calls,
even the social worker consulted

for our "special" son
and dancing between broccoli

or spinach for dinner. Nothing
glamorous about that

only somehow we are
until one of us stumbles

and the clouds give out,
water collapsing down,

a regular torrent with knives
flashing across sky,

more now, I can see than
simple table sprinklings,

pooling everywhere into lakes,
disappearing the furniture,

drowning shapes, washing,
swallowing everything up

while somewhere
someone won't stop bleeding.

DEAD WRONG

I never dreamed I could lose so much sleep
that year the blanket stitched in scarlet

wouldn't stop my daughter from crying
no matter how tight I swaddled her.

Heater cranked to full,
nights went icy with waking terrors.

I'd wait and pray for smooth passage,
doze to the television erupting

updates on desert invasions
while green fingers of budding lilies

clawed dirt in the dark outside. Fatigued
treks next day to the supermarket

meant surreal seas of people
I'd thought were smart,

taken to be kind, in cars pimped
with flags pummeling the wind

as they sped past, windshields
beating a flashy red, white and blue.

Perfume of petroleum
and night-blooming Jasmine,

doomed dictators
and fresh-baked cookies,

my breasts two fat burros
sweating milk under Maidenform.

And maybe they were kind—
I don't know—

except the haunting thwack
of flags lingered—how

could they not hear it?
The rest of us swayed with candles,

held vigils against warring hawks,
their mechanism unchained.

Twelve years later and see how
dead wrong they were.

Women grovel for grain
and a scrap of shade,

the hot blur of beaks
bears down. Trish,

I'll never forget your calls
from Connecticut, mornings

you'd drop the kids and stand
with signs on the overpass:

War is still not healthy
for children and other living things

held up to a sharp spring sky,
to a few shy smiles, though

mostly honks, foul-mouthed
zingers and *Fuck-You* gifs

clashing on the bridge
around you, high-fives

morphed to raised fists
clutching cardboard grenades

of half-consumed Starbucks,
the white rockets

commuters would hurl, splattering
shadows across the highway,

that like all matter plied
with enough force and heat,

in time, disappear.

F O O D

Tastes good when you are willing to put some muscle into making it, willing to stand for a sweaty eternity in the indestructible Doc Martens restaurant chefs wear slicing green onions and celery root until their hands bleed clean through thick oak. Eventually, you learn how much force and saffron, precision and mire poix are needed to make soup for the masses sing. Sometimes it's easier to feed others than face what's eating you. *We're hungry, we're so hungry* the modern radio rocker confessed as I cruised here this morning to confront my double Americano and the empty plate of a blank notebook. Writing, which is like eating and vomiting at the same time in a regal sort of way. Ask Louis XIV who loved to eat and died with a stomach stretched galaxies wider than what the organs orbiting it required. Just ask the World Health Organization how if not for hoarders there's plenty for everyone. Louis and his love affair with strawberries. And Versailles! The endless fields he planted so organic farmers of the future could dream like Lilliputians, like tiny seed people slung in the yellow hammocks of blooming asparagus. The agony of Antoinette who mistook The People for layers of Chantilly cream-plumped pastry she could chow down and not choke. Food. Let them eat it. Let them make it themselves! And decades of meat-grinding revolutions later, that's exactly what they did, everyone in Paris armed with their own Escoffier bible, everyone a king in a paper toque, plotting gratin take-overs, kick-ass Hollandaise and wicked veloutes, sitting at table with Toulouse Lautrec who loved dining and cafes and spiking his guests' water pitchers with gold fish so his palette could not be diluted. Gertrude Stein and Alice B. feeding friends magic brownies as establishment walls toppled, everything tasting peculiar: surreal, slanted, strange, the new order seen from delirious heights and yet in spite of Stein, Picasso, Dali, the eventual Model T, Cuisinarts, God Particles and so-called Democracy, we're still recipes short of sating hoards of unfed souls, miles of empty bellies extended if we could just get the grain lockers there, turn constellations of want, of gaping oral anti-matter into starry satisfaction. Mick Jagger knew and pretty much everyone walking around knows that sometimes you just can't get none aside from a few Wise Ones in sandals and saffron robes tramping the globe, hippies in hills off the Oregon Coast where creeks merge into castle turrets of towering Redwoods, where people feed on silence and are nourished by the moon's simple choreography across a July night sky, veils of luminous cumulus like gods signaling from far off to me, to you, and though it may make no difference, to the girl stuck somewhere in a far-off field, her chapped feet chained to brittle roots of no rain, to the earth's barren core, girl with bones thin as smoke, the moon but a harsh white spotlight on her hand as it passes over her mouth like a shadow, a sigh, a yawn, an exit sign of exhaustion, of no satisfaction, of trying not to think maybe this is the end.

IN THE DAWN OF THE COMING AUTUMN YOU WILL GREET US, TRIUMPHANT OR INSIDE THE QUEENDOM OF DELIGHTS

You who rise from darkening leaves
the lambent filament
gold about your temples

Who bring bold meat to the slaughter
yet harm no creatures
in the making of your mind

Your figures always drawn
with stars and sparks
streaming from their eyes

Little songstress
still wanders the house
your mouth an open cloud

For us to float on
we who erase ourselves
inside succulent refrains

Our brash muscles flexed
atop the ruins of the day
for which you sound

A lyric tonic
launched from inked lips
that other dimension

Will the code begin to fade
with your body's bloom
its growing moon

Of wishful prescriptions
the calculated risk
of your flesh flown to full?

Or unveil a vine invincible
signing from unchained heights
our lady of the infinite imagined

J A R

The genius of glass, to allow two things at once.

Worlds squirming inside molten sand
        and lime: butterflies,
           marmalade, pennies, gauze—baggage

savory and sweet, stamped with ecstasy and grief
and seen through the lens
of a breakable terrain.

I have reached the part where no thing gleams,

heralding necessary artifice, a switching of
Day for Night.

Like Rachel had to conceal
        the symbolic bag, sweating it out
        atop token treasure, her skirt a tent,
        tented glass. Daughter,

we hoard
the moon, the stars—nothing else
needed out here

where walls turn black
        and we roam a free landscape
        of wild radiance

seeded in Love's tender tufts.
Consider the trickery it takes

to keep grass tended, greening
and graciously. The heart

has its own breed of currency:
I crown you keeper of the mint.

You who learn to be fluent
in languages

we've invented in our sleep.

ROLLING BALL WRITER

This pitch plastic wand
scratches the page
tapered streamlined
to say
what I tell it
Do you want to hear something sweet?
Is it going to fly up in flames?
Have you longed to taste
that place called
Gasoline
the past we keep running through
sage hills soaked
with birds
shaping a dark hat
Tippi Hedren style
I know her
Eucalyptus-laced
smacking of mints
and bitter fennel
Why don't you
rustle the leaves
we can recall
jack-rabbit signs
flurries of dust
kicked up behind
tender anise castles
the weird looking spindles
and that queen
in the left-wing window
her hair a red flag

signaling baby fish below
diadems
bobbing on the surface
a moat on fire
You're doing it again
making black licorice
spank your tongue
pretending a pen
could crack those squawking sounds
like magic candy stings
wings and claws
scratching wet ink
leaking strange news
all over
your messy mouth

FREE

I'm lucky to have
this bistro table and stool, the kids
at school, time before market and shuttling
to lessons, Office Depot
for Pink Pearl erasers, colored chalk.
Even better would be
to score that awesome residency,
a room by the sea in a dead movie star's house,
far from the hiss and grind
of baristas shoveling beans, steaming
rush hour milk,
Rufus Wainwright crooning on hidden loop
inside buckled walls. I could laugh
or slit my meaningless wrists
not that it's funny thinking about
last year's residency pick, the Persian poet
whose wife lost her head
to a fascist regime, really,
what do I know of suffering?
If there were times wandering
the mall, sobbing into my fries
I thought of Paris, running free
from debt, sick children,
a stressed-out tryst, so what?
In the stubbled turret of the Hotel Esmeralda
I'd disappear, send smoke signals
up my rickety flue. They'd shoot past
Notre Dame, over ancient
hobbled streets, a disembodied moon
and still the gargoyles frozen
to their indifferent haunches
would grimace back, unmoved.

LUPERCALIA

The ides of February are brutal.
Love's sticky sentiments
gumming up the air
make it harder
to breathe. Gilded truffles
snug in their cellophane tombs
dare you to pluck them
from underworlds
and eat. Hearts dangle
in pharmacy windows
pretending to pump real red.
Brutal for a boy who feels
but won't say
what it is to be sixteen
and never one secret admirer,
never a glitter doily
or silver Hallmark
waxed with lipstick's
smoky kisses. What ghost
can this mother conjure?
What diaphanous caress?
When in Rome
and if long ago, I could run
naked through alley ways,
my breasts swinging
like fevered trolls,
like devil bells bared,
tolling resident evil. I could
don a goat-skin cap,
carry my pot

of flames to the desert,
burn salted meal-cakes
with vestal virgins
and raise them
to the stars,
to dead crows
and broken Caesars. But
it wouldn't change the fact
of his incomplete beauty,
how girls turn away
when he opens his mouth to speak
a sound less than smart.
Won't change the fact
of his gawky bust
and uncommon sense,
an art far too wild
and no longer cradled
in the cave of a darkened living room,
where once we rocked
and he suckled, at times, stopped
to let glide
the nipple from his mouth
and look up at me,
        just look at me...
his future,
his mother
and unconditional lover,
his only Valentine.

When he motors the window down,
a breeze-warmed broth flows through,
citrus mix of budding orange blossoms
and his own growing spice:
groin and pit, he can't help touching
with fingers to sniff. Awkward innocent,
shoulders even with mine
and muscle-ripe,
he could snap the neck of a bird,
any one of the inmates
in this obsolete aviary
where we arrive to find
skeleton cages, furry
with iron filings, rust residue.
Where have they gone,
the Chinese Geese, Blue Crown Conures,
our Love Birds from Australia?
We turn to salute
the squalling present: one testy
Sri-Lankan Peacock drags
his tapered brilliance towards us,
flashes an azure wave and flees.
Run-of-the-mill pigeons flutter,
a white parrot cries *Hello! Hello!*
to the upturned curve
of my son's smile. No longer
hormonal-nuts, I hardly recognize him,
alien as this scrappy state park,
its lifeline clamped in fiscal-skittish hands.
Hello! Hello! it shrieks again,

our friend hung out
like a rare sun, an albino honeydew
on his jail swing, singing. Neruda
knew beauty banked
in the commonest things:
splayed feather, empty chair,
the emperor's torn socks
stepping under the guillotine,
a coin in the gutter, spinning. Knew how
the skull of a coconut split
births blue islands,
this milky dream we share
in the ruined shadows of a cage, condemned
to love what's left
and what's no longer there.

SAVIOR

A horse jumped the fence somewhere in Devon
and bolted for the forest
bringing traffic to a halt on the crowded highway.
No one expected what happened next:
mini van of string quartet players
unfolded onto asphalt—black-clad bandits
with their strung gut, their polished bodies
of sanded willow, they began to strum
and drivers tumbled forth to listen
like the children of Hamlin. Spellbound
in wildflowers and grass,
weepy to Pachebel's Canon in D,
favorite air of weddings
and solemn ceremonies.
What's beyond necessary
need not be sought: a divided road, a falling sun,
fair setting for the exceptional.
Who will be called to save the world?
No one knows
but the beast rides farther into green,
its mane trembling to a violin's vibrato.
Know this:
the doctor must always be in.
Someone always there to sing the horse home.

WIND

BECAUSE

Because the night belongs to lovers
—PATTI SMITH

And felines and cat-like
you stalk shadows, unraveling
everything in the house tonight:
bustier lace, dark nipples
of rain, their plum curves
pressed to the window
as the curl of something feral
flirts under curtain. You're
naked, the bed, our boat
and bent over my body's glass,
the moon through the slats
makes milk of its surface,
your tongue to the waves
cast deep as you rise
and the willow groans outside
in a stiff wind. I had no idea
how far down I was,
what igneous caves ran,
flaming orange
in my Barrier Reef, my underworld,
my Mauna Kea,
until you showed me
the mountain head, the raw stone
glowing, my buried gold
giving up its hottest
story—bronze posse
of feminine feet released,
running wild—high grass

and the whole wide land
at once, *oh God*,
rippling, rippling, rippling.

MOBY DICK INDIVIDUATION

The story grows larger with each passing
page. The cannibal passes time, counting
pages in a pew like a child counts stars.
One falls and sizzles, lost to black water.
Sometimes a pipe is really a coffin, but a sign buried
bodes well for second comings. I bite down,
my bone leg propped in place. The whale,
a captain roped to her crucifix—wind and entrails
of a compass lashed around white teeth. Becoming
becomes me; I'm afraid of I don't know
what. Time and a throat that dries, pried open
in awe. My head made of blubber, light
for a thousand lamps. Sheen of milked sky
and this new moon rising as my old code fades,
flashed from shore. Once, I stood before the wave,
the monster breaching. What could I do
but dive straight for it? When the first myth dies,
my red flag opens, a tenderest void. Harpoon thrust,
the frighted air, and then the heart, burst.

HORSEY

Of the Mary Poppins carousel.
Red and white candy stripes,
Dick Van Dyke. Black bee
and the stung Mustang
that chucked me in a ditch
near a river snaking through Northern California.
I have a certain respect
for a creature that drags me by one stirrup
as my ribs rake dirt. Field song of sticks
and stones blazing the washboard
of my back. It was love at first flight
I tell you and I lived
to fall again. Horse head
in the Godfather nightmare,
the red streams gushing
under sleek white sheets. High
horse with flared breath,
snorting nostrils, the sweaty
flanks and tail painting
erect skies umber
as the devil sails through space,
kicking up dust and snails. Show pony,
work nag. Smiling metal
of the hammered shoe.
The blessing of mud
because times are best
when a little messy and dangerous.
I believe in a domination of clouds.
I prefer to be fearless
but I'll submit I'm an animal

doing the mystery dance
just like everyone else
in my mane of many veils;
my neck a long gate
swinging open to greet you; the wind
that insists on
swapping secrets with your eyes.

BLACKFISH

I don't know what to make of the world-class trainer
who rode the bulbous rostrum of great Tilikum—stroking,
smooching, snuggling it goodnight—a thousand times
letting that god Orca toss her skywards—bright coin
tumbled back on blue pools that rippled open
like chakras on an amusement park pond. Applause
must have been narcotic, veins of diver and fish
synchronized to claps and commands until one day
he turned and bit in, her shape in that moment
so much chum to him. Some forces are drawn
to firelight and some are born to endless night
as the slow spins of the tarantella thrum
and the poet slumps to tile with a spike in his arm. Shadows
will consume live flesh given enough dungeons
to fume in, like mother yeast yields the bread of Nirvana
in a cloaked bowl and sponges bloom in vinegar bottles
left to gather dust on a kitchen shelf. Festering has its upside
when you consider the wings of a sherry wine butterfly
cocooned in pitch wet. Therein, Duende lies,
sickly sweet as ground up flowers
from a funeral parlor floor. We light candles for the dead,
clear space for pallbearers weaving another casket
through wind and rain, a Leviathan on stilts, its box
shined up to glow though we know it's hard as wood. And still
voices rush in, saying *lean closer* from water's edge,
closer to better view our eeriest reflections, magnificence
moving dark and monstrous beneath a surface thinner than skin.

LION ATTACKING A HORSE

—sculpture, Greek, 325-300 BCE

Three tons of porous marble flown high
over continents on wind
and Getty purse strings
after twenty centuries parked in Rome.
Stallions mauled by noble beasts
in Hellenistic worlds
were sign of the times: emperors and generals
playing God with the little people. Here,
one walks in circles under domed atrium light,
faint fish aromas whipped in
on Malibu sea breezes. The way
that lion's claws scrape shady
indents in the stallion's stone side,
you'd think time had stopped forever,
the still-pulsing steed stilled
by a sculptor's lean chisel. Read how
loving mentees of Michelangelo
mended severed heads years later
with their fine Renaissance hands. Before that,
Circus Maximus lured it home
until stairwells of the Palazzo
made it *mise en scène* for the fatally sentenced.
Show me an art unstained by blood.
I'd be lying if I claimed exemption.
There's a poem in here somewhere
and I'll kill what I have to to get it.

Has less to do with money
or the acquisition of goods
that Wind of Paradise
an exclusive fist
of pink Himalayan salt
can topple you
it's painful to watch
the legs lose their kick
angel wings flail
so much depends
on a single slow breath
scrubbed in austerity
beside the chicken
begging water
in red rain
two coins gently placed
on the eyes' ribbed duvets
two doors pulled down
a choice to walk through
like Teiresias was unique
having lived as woman and man
the world suddenly opens
and our mayor rides
into town: Dionysus
the mask without borders
flesh and ether bleeding
into one diamond flame
that blinds
as it makes and breaks

No one here cares
if you lose your head
and drift off
even the beetles love to be trampled
six feet down
they're slathering their pits
in mud honey
promising songs to burn brighter
beneath the deafening roll
of coming, stampeding hooves

APHRODITE IN LOS ANGELES

Her hair was crazy with wind,
her face animated with chatter.

We slogged through a sea
of backed-up traffic,

bright baubles flashing
in the August heat.

Hands clamped to the wheel,
I drove on, determined to deliver

that goddess on time,
her fans across town gathering

at the brick university to hear
the hymns of praise. Between flurries

of words she'd pause,
lift an American Spirit

to her famous red pucker
and suck in, white smoke

curling around the cabin,
clouding my eyes

as she held her lens up
to the landscape and clicked:

a house she claimed
was shaped like a ship,

the manhole a mandala
inked in strange writing,

a Great Dane at the signal,
its proud snout sniffing hot air.

Beauty! She cried. *There's so much
beauty in the world — just look at it!*

And I did, though I could not yet see
what she saw, did not understand

the urgency in her voice
had little to do with getting there,

only a swatch of sky
in that window behind her

filling with gold and copper
light, glowing fiercer

as the sun went down
and distant wildfires raged on

in the sacred mountains San Bernardino.

JONI MITCHELL IS NOT UNCONSCIOUS!

She hasn't fallen into the coma
those nasty tabloids suggest
She's alert and well and sitting up
in her bed at Cedars Sinai
I was walking on The Promenade
in the land of palm trees and Saint Monica
where sun and blue shade duke it out
wending a path between bass clef and treble
and then I saw it: JONI MITCHELL IN A COMA!
And I said No! Not her! Maybe it's true
she's been a recluse for half the century
in her pink Bel-Air mansion
Our Lady of the Spanish Canyon
where she chain smokes and is paranoid of everybody
especially the invisible parasites
like *colorful irritable fibers*
she's convinced bloody her skin
make her tear all her clothes off
and slither like wind on ceramic tiles
Who wouldn't believe aliens
were camping in your private parts
when there's Paparazzi spying
from the Hydrangea everywhere you go?
There is no rain in California
and I have been to Hollywood parties
and done perfectly disgraceful things
But Joni Mitchell is not unconscious!
She is still here in the in-between
going up and down like her melodies
make us when the heart is shadows and light
and we are desperate to be forgiven
Oh Joni keep singing we need that nothing gray about you

I DON'T WANT A FUNERAL

I've no desire to be tucked into the ordered bricks of the family
columbarium, much as I love that church with its medieval pipes and
every Easter the lunatic Wisteria overrun by black bee asylums high
on weeping nectar. Not even its original prayer garden that survived
the big fire of '76 can sell me such burial. Not the carved statue of St.
Francis, his cheek nuzzled by attendant deer, not the dove on his sleeve
tweeting Good News, not the giant gnarled sycamores we'd climb like
mythological squid—jungle gyms that hefted us high and away over the
city. Once we snuck into the sacristy and consumed sacraments off hours.
I knew where priests hid the key and feeling for the cold nail under the
sink where they'd lean to brace and baptize themselves, eyes pep-talked
out of weary in the chipped mirror at Big Game time. So many souls to
boost, spirits to raise, the dead one more day. It feels almighty when it's
all holy all the time, even that naughty me and my sidekick, Velma, more
along for my mischievous ride, reaching for what didn't belong to us. We
never drank the wine; it was the bread we were after. Fistfuls crammed
against tongues, burying our teeth in a pile of hosts tasting faintly of
cardboard, each stamped, dead center, with miniature crosses, pasty in
my palm, perfect signs to match my nervous lines, life-veins, fortune. I
swallowed tall stacks, wanting to be saved—self-service, sacrificial. We're
only human and sometimes standing in the kitchen late at night with
my husband, our hands and tongues groping, grabbing whole moons of
him from behind, I think of past plunders, how there's still something
supernatural about hunger after so many years and how sometimes I'd
like him to fuck me in all my places at once—fingers, cock, tongue—a
gymnasium of pleasure, my mouth a knight lusting for unknown grail.
I'll repeat: don't bury me. Not when what I want is to take it all in and
zip up, disappeared. To reject marker, being marked, bound, plotted,
arrested. Isn't death enough of an impediment? We burn and there's an
uncontrollable fire, and then containers for ashes arrive in the mail. I

tried to cram the Holy Ghost into my mouth, daring parents, the men
in robes to catch me. Deliver me transparency, a slow wind and shift to
invisible. Like Jesus and Claude Rains only showed form, bound by gauze
and then unraveling. No, when I die, make a little boat and let me out,
my sails set to sea, my dust launched to a red horizon. This ashen tongue
will lick the sun and dissolve, remembering its place: first flesh to taste
and last to forget the bread, the cup, this body risen in light.

EPILOGUE

EPIPHANY II

Then one morning you woke early,
struck by a strange knowing,
a risen voice repeating:

The soul of the soul of the soul is love.

And you walked outside in your red flannel pj's,
little white Terrier dogs wrapped in blue plaid scarves
dancing on the sleeves
and looking up
saw the still dark sky
lit with a few bright stars.

ACKNOWLEDGEMENTS

Grateful acknowledgement is made to the following publications in which these poems first appeared: *The American Poetry Review*: "The Goods"; *BTWN*: "Portal to an Ephemeral Elsewhere," "Recycled Coliseum" *Connotation Press*: "Elegy for a Body," "Gold Silk Spiders," "Resentment is a Hard Habit to Break"; Cultural Weekly: "Lion Attacking a Horse"; "When the Sky Makes a Certain Sign"; *diode*: "A Hole Opens Up in the Middle of the Day," "Dressed Up Like Holmes, Falling Into a Glass Darkly," "Food" "How Like Marriage is the Season of Flowers," "In the Beginning, Somewhat Elevated," "Then I Let You Go"; *Konundrum Engine Literary Review*: "With Take Another Piece of My Heart Now, Baby..."; *Life and Legends*: "Gold Ring," "Rolling Ball Writer"; *Linebreak*: "Because," "Joni Mitchell is not Unconscious"; *The Long Islander (Walt's Corner)*: "Epiphany II"; *Manor House Quarterly*: "I Don't Want a Funeral"; *Narrative Magazine*: "The Couple Who Fell to Earth"; *The Paris-American*: "Moby Dick Individuation"; *Poemeleon*: "Finding Steckel Park With My Son," "Morning at the Cafe Vida"

"The Couple Who Fell to Earth" was a semi-finalist for the 2014 Rita Dove
 Poetry Award
"The Goods" takes the reigns from the inimitable Wendell Berry's "Goods"
"How Like Marriage is the Season of Flowers" inspired by James Merrill's
 "Cloud Country"
"Immanent, Purgatorio" incorporates random phrases and words from
 Dante Alighieri's *The Divine Comedy*, translated by Allen
 Mandelbaum
"Joni Mitchell is not Unconscious!" takes its cue from "Poem [Lana Turner
 Has Collapsed]" by Frank O'Hara

"The Couple Who Fell to Earth" is for Phil Abrams
"Nemesis Necklace" is for Meg LeFauve
"Dressed Up Like Holmes, Falling Into a Glass Darkly" is for Tom Diggs
"Gold Ring" is for Richard Bitting

"In the Dawn of the Coming Autumn You Will Greet Us Triumphant..." is
    for Margaret Stohl
"Aphrodite in Los Angeles" is for Dorianne Laux

Deep gratitude to my children, my Phil Abrams, my Dorianne Laux and Joseph Millar, James Meetze (for making it beautiful), Jason Katims, Brother John, my myth cohorts and profs at Pacifica, my parents, but mostly, my husband Phil Abrams for all his hard work, lively parenting and patience seeing me through this wicked adventure. *Pax Aeterna*.